Bizarre Birds

Bizarre Birds

Sara Swan Miller

Watts LIBRARY

Franklin Watts
A Division of Grolier Publishing
New York • London • Hong Kong • Sydney
Danbury, Connecticut

Note to readers: Definitions for words in **bold** can be found in the Glossary at the back of this book.

Photographs ©: BBC Natural History Unit: 26 (John Cancalosi), 22 (Ashish Chandola); Brian Kenney: 5 bottom, 10, 20, 21, 49, 50; Dembinsky Photo Assoc.: 6 (Doug Locke), 43 (Fritz Polking); ENP Images/Gerry Ellis: 14, 38; Kevin Schafer: 2, 18, 28; Peter Arnold Inc.: 15, 30, 31 (Luiz C. Marigo), 5 top, 34 (Michael Sewell), 46, 47 (Gunter Ziesler); Photo Researchers: 29 (George Holton), 24 (M.P. Kahl), 36, 37 (Anthony Mercieca); Stone: cover (Paul Kenward), 8 (Manoj Shah), 13 (Steve Vidler), 40, 41 (Art Wolfe); Visuals Unlimited: 16 (Ken Lucas), 44, 45 (Rick Poley).

The photograph on the cover shows a family of ostriches walking along the road. The photograph opposite the title page shows a group of emperor penguins tobogganing across the ice.

Visit Franklin Watts on the Internet at:
http://publishing.grolier.com

Library of Congress Cataloging-in-Publication Data

Miller, Sara Swan
    Bizarre Birds / by Sara Swan Miller
        p.   cm.— (Watts Library)
    Includes bibliographical references and index.
    Summary: Discusses several species of birds that have unusual appearances, habitats, or behavior, such as the ostrich, jacana, and toucan.
    ISBN 0-531-11796-6 (lib. bdg.)   0-531-13981-6 (pbk.)
    1. Birds—Juvenile literature. [1. Birds.] I. Title. II. Series.
QL676.2.M56 2000
598—dc21
                                          99-057282

Contents

Chapter One
What Is a Bird? 7

Chapter Two
Birds That Can't Fly 11

Chapter Three
Where's Your Nest? 21

Chapter Four
What a Strange Way to Act! 31

Chapter Five
Weird Beaks and Feathers 39

Chapter Six
Fine Feathered Finale 51

53 **Bizarre Birds Around the World**

55 **Glossary**

57 **To Find Out More**

60 **A Note on Sources**

61 **Index**

Robins look and act the way that birds are "supposed" to look and act.

Chapter One

What Is a Bird?

Of course you know what a bird is. You see robins, sparrows, crows, and pigeons all the time. You might even know someone who has a pet bird, such as a parakeet or a finch. Maybe you've learned the "rules" that separate birds from other groups, or classes, of animals, so you know how birds are different from insects, amphibians, reptiles, and mammals. Suppose your teacher asked you to describe a bird. What would you say?

First, you would probably say that a bird has feathers and can fly. You might add that birds build nests and lay eggs. You might go on to say that birds are **warm blooded** animals that can maintain their own body temperature and don't need the sun's heat to keep their bodies warm enough to move. They are **vertebrates**, animals that have backbones.

Over many years, birds have developed special adaptations for flying. Birds need to be lightweight to fly easily. They have beaks that are lightweight but still quite strong, instead of the heavy jaws that many other animals have. Bird bones are hol-

The Biggest Bird

The ostrich of Africa may stand 9 feet (2.7 meters) tall. It would tower over the tallest person!

low, which saves weight. Bird feathers are also light but strong, and bird bodies are streamlined so that the air slips over them in flight. Instead of arms, they have wings. They have strong flying muscles that help them flap their wings. These muscles attach to a large, blade-like bone, called a **keel**, on their breastbone.

Most birds rely on their keen eyesight and good hearing to find food, locate their mates, and escape from danger. Their sense of smell is less well developed.

Finally, most birds lay small **clutches** of hard-shelled eggs in their nests. They sit on their eggs to keep them warm, and, after the eggs hatch, adult birds usually care for the young until they're ready to go off on their own.

If you said all that, your teacher would probably be pleased—but you wouldn't be entirely correct. Do *all* birds fly? Do *all* birds have keen eyesight? Do *all* birds make nests and sit on their eggs? The surprising answer is "No!"

The world of birds has plenty of exceptions to every rule. Some birds don't look the way they're "supposed" to look, or act the way we expect them to act. Now, let's find out more about these fascinating birds!

The Tiniest Bird

The tiny bee hummingbird of South America is only 2¼ inches (5.7 cm) long. It's smaller than many moths!

This woodpecker is a strong flier—but not all birds are.

Chapter Two

Birds That Can't Fly?

When you think of a bird, you probably picture a feathered creature soaring through the air. Maybe you imagine a robin, a bluejay, or a woodpecker flitting from tree to tree. When most of us think "bird," we think "flying." We usually don't think of a large bird running along the ground. If you do try to imagine a flightless bird, you may think of an ostrich, but the ostrich isn't the only bird that can't get off the ground. Over millions of years, several species of birds have lost the ability to fly. Instead of having the big **keel** that flying birds have, these birds have flat breastbones. Their wings have become small and useless for flying. However, these birds are well adapted for a life on the ground. They don't *need* to fly anymore!

The Flightless Kiwi

This odd-looking ball of fluff doesn't really look much like a bird. The only bird-like things about it are a long bill, two scaly legs, and two little feet poking out from its shaggy, hair-like feathers. Where are its wings? Where is its tail? What kind of bird has such a small head?

Actually, the kiwi does have wings, but they are very small and hidden under its feathers. Like other flightless birds, it has no keel on its breastbone and no strong muscles for flying. A kiwi couldn't fly if its life depended on it!

These strange little kiwis have their own ways of staying safe. To begin with, they smell bad, so many predators aren't interested in eating them. They hide in burrows during the day, where it's hard for their enemies to find them. If they are attacked, they swiftly scurry away on their sturdy legs. Although kiwis are only as big as a chicken, they can outrun a human. Its legs are good for more than running. If a kiwi is cornered, it will lash out with its feet.

Kiwis live in the forests of New Zealand, and they come out only at night to hunt for berries, insects, snails, and worms. You might expect them to have large eyes like an owl

This little spotted kiwi has two eggs in its nest. Often, the kiwi will only lay one.

to help them see in the dark, but kiwis have small eyes and poor vision. So how does a kiwi find its food?

Unlike all other birds, a kiwi has nostrils on the tip of its beak, and it has an excellent sense of smell! It also has special

A Fast Runner

The emu of Australia can't fly either, but it can run away from its enemies at up to 30 miles (48 kilometers) per hour.

sensory bristles around the base of its long, probing bill that help it locate its food.

The kiwi has another claim to fame. The female kiwi often lays only one egg. Female birds of other species lay usually several eggs. However, the one egg that a female kiwi lays is much larger than those of any other bird her size. A kiwi egg weighs one-sixth of the adult female's total body weight. Imagine if a chicken laid eggs that weighed 1.5 pounds (0.6 kilograms)! That single, large kiwi egg has all the nutrients needed to feed the developing **embryo**. It takes eleven weeks for the egg to hatch, the longest **incubation period** of any bird. Then, only a week after it hatches, the young kiwi hops out of its burrow and begins hunting for its own food.

The Endangered Rhea

You can't miss a rhea running across the plains of South America. It stands up to 5 feet tall (1.5 m) on its long, muscular legs. A rhea can't fly, but it has no trouble escaping from predators. It can run up to 40 miles (64 km) per hour. That's faster than the fastest horse!

The rhea has unusually long wings for a flightless bird. It uses them like airplane rudders to help it twist and turn as it runs. Once a rhea is grown, it doesn't have many enemies—except humans. People kill rheas for their skins, which they make into leather. They also use their feathers to make feather dusters. In addition, people hunt rheas for their meat and for the oil they produce. Rheas will devour almost any crop that a farmer plants, so many farmers kill them on sight.

A puna rhea puts on the speed in this Chilean desert.

15

Their numbers have steadily decreased, and they are now threatened with **extinction**. Some day there may be no more rheas.

Rheas are odd birds in another way. The male rhea mates with as many as twelve females, and they all lay their eggs in a nest he has built. Each female lays a single egg every other day for up to 10 days. After the male starts sitting on the nest, the females lay more eggs nearby. The male scrapes them into his nest with his wing or his bill. Then the females go off to find other mates, leaving the male to sit on the eggs. He may have as many as sixty eggs to take care of!

This male rhea has a lot of eggs to care for.

What Good is Being Flightless?

Over time, a surprising number of birds have lost the ability to fly. How could a bird benefit from not being able to fly? Believe it or not, being flightless has its advantages. A flightless bird doesn't need to develop and carry large flight muscles, or have to burn up the energy that flying requires. So a flightless bird can get by with less food, and can survive in places where food is scarce.

Of course, there is a disadvantage too. A flightless bird is more likely to be attacked and eaten by predators. That explains why flightless birds have **evolved** in places where there are fewer enemies. Kiwis, for instance, were once safe in New Zealand. After people brought predators from other countries to New Zealand, kiwis were endangered. They are now threatened with extinction.

When the chicks hatch, the male rhea cares for them. He teaches them what to eat and where to find water. The male rhea is a good guardian of the young. He protects them from wolves and other enemies, and even from female rheas that come too close. He kicks out fiercely with his feet, slashing intruders with his big, sharp toenails.

A male rhea guarding chicks will even attack a human who comes too near. Ranchers herding their sheep know to stay well away from nesting rheas!

The Biggest Bird, The Ostrich

Ostriches are not only the biggest birds in the world, but also the heaviest. They can weigh up to 350 pounds (150 kg). Scientists say that no bird that weighs more than 40 pounds (18 kg) can fly, because it could never have enough muscle

A male and female ostrich in Kenya.

strength to get off the ground. Obviously, ostriches are way over the weight limit!

Ostriches are well suited to life on the ground. With their long, muscular legs they can run up to 45 miles (72 km) an hour. That's even faster than a lion. Ostriches race along on the tips of their two toes. If one of these big birds is cornered, it lashes out with its heavy, horny claws.

Ostriches live in dry areas in Africa, where there is very little to eat or drink. They can survive for a long time without drinking water if there are moist plants to eat, and they can travel long distances to search for food. They eat mostly plants—but not just any plant will do. They prefer seed heads of grasses and certain flowers. For such a big bird, an ostrich has a surprisingly delicate beak, so it can pick up exactly the seed it wants. Of course, when an ostrich is feeding on low-growing plants, predators could easily sneak up on it, so a feeding ostrich must raise its head often to look around for danger.

Ostriches have some unusual nesting habits. The male mates with several females. All the females lay their eggs in the same nest, and one dominant female, usually the oldest, guards all the eggs during the day. The ostrich is the only bird that willingly takes care of other females' eggs. However, if there are too many eggs for the dominant female to keep warm, she pushes the eggs laid by the other females out of the nest. She never pushes out her own eggs. All ostrich eggs may look the same to us, but a mother ostrich somehow knows which eggs are hers.

Have you ever heard that ostriches bury their heads in the sand when danger comes? That is not true, but they do something that is almost as strange. When it wants to hide, an ostrich will sometimes lie on the ground with its long neck stretched out flat. Maybe it feels as if it's invisible!

The Biggest Bird Ever

The flightless elephant bird, which is now extinct, would have towered over the ostrich. It weighed about 1000 pounds (450 kg), and its egg was huge too. Seven big ostrich eggs would fit inside one elephant bird's egg! Elephant birds died out 400 years ago, but people still find pieces of their tough-shelled eggs.

A bald eagle sits on its huge stick nest.

Chapter Three

Where's Your Nest?

Where would you look for birds' nests? You might check high up among the branches of a tree or bush, or in holes in tree trunks. You might look under the eaves of buildings in your neighborhood or inside a birdhouse in your yard. You might search for nests on the ground or hidden down in burrows. Some birds, though, make their nests in places you would never think of—even in water! In fact, some birds don't even make nests at all, but they still manage to protect their eggs. These unusual birds have developed their own ways of keeping their eggs safe and warm.

The Pheasant-Tailed Jacana

Jacanas lay their eggs on water! They build their simple nests on top of floating plants in the marshes where they live. Most of the time the nests stay afloat, but sometimes a nest that is a bit too heavy sinks a little. When those chicks hatch, they are in for a wet surprise! They have to climb onto water lilies to dry out in the sun.

This pheasant-tailed jacana has built a nest in a swamp.

Jacanas are odd in another way too. Most birds have only one mate at a time. Some male birds, such as kiwis and ostriches, may mate with several females. Jacana females mate with several males, and the males take care of the eggs and the young. One female may mate with as many as ten different males, and she lays four eggs in each clutch. Forty eggs would be a lot of eggs to take care of if the female jacana didn't spread the job around between many males!

Some people say that jacanas walk about with their eggs under their wings to incubate them, but this story is only partly true. When an African jacana's eggs or chicks are in danger, the male may tuck them under his wings and run away. Most of the time, though, the eggs stay in their watery nest.

If you ever saw jacanas in a marsh, you might think they were walking on water. It does look that way, but jacanas are actually walking on floating leaves or water lilies. Their very long toes spread their weight out so that they don't sink into the water. In fact, some people call them "lily trotters."

Jacanas Around the World

There are seven species of jacanas. They live in tropical areas in Africa, India, Southeast Asia, New Guinea, Australia, and the Americas.

The Shaft-Tailed Whydah

The shaft-tailed whydahs of Africa have a great labor-saving device. They don't bother to make nests of their own. They simply lay their eggs in another bird's nest and fly away!

Not just any nest will do, however. Shaft-tailed whydahs always lay their eggs in the nests of violet-eared waxbills. The newly hatched whydahs have the same mouth markings and calls as young waxbills, so waxbill parents can't tell the difference between the hatchlings. They raise all the chicks as if they were their own. Meanwhile, the whydah parents can spend their days loafing and feeding, while someone else does all the work.

Shaft-tailed whydahs were named for their showy tails. During breeding season, the males grow long, drooping tail feathers. They put on a very elaborate dance, looping and soaring in the air, with their long tail feathers fluttering out behind them. The male with the best display wins the female.

A male shaft-tailed whydah shows off his tail feathers.

After mating, though, the males lose their long tails and grow plain new feathers that match those of the females. With plainer feathers, they are harder to see and they are safer foraging for food on the ground. They can fly more easily without the long tails too.

A whydah has a startling way of searching for seeds on the ground. It scratches the ground while jumping straight up with both feet. It looks more like a wind-up toy than a real bird.

The Mallee Fowl

When it comes to taking care of eggs, the mallee fowl of Australia has its own tried-and-true method. It doesn't build a nest or sit on its eggs. Instead, the male builds a big mound of rotting vegetation for the female to lay her eggs in.

If you've ever built a compost pile in your yard, you know that the inside of a pile of rotting leaves can get warm. As the leaves in the pile are broken down by bacteria for food, those microscopic organisms give off heat. The mallee fowl uses the heat from its mound to keep eggs just the right temperature.

During the winter the male collects leaves and bark. He digs out the center of the mound and adds the leaf litter. When the rains come, the leaves begin to rot and give off heat. He covers the mound with soil and sand to keep in the heat. In the spring, when the temperature is just right, the female lays up to thirty-five eggs in the mound and covers them with leaves.

Cuckoo Criminals

Cuckoos also lay their eggs in other birds' nests. Often, the big cuckoo chick even pushes the chicks of the nest builders out of the nest.

This male mallee fowl is working on his nest mound.

Thanks for the Volcano

The common scrub fowl, a relative of the mallee fowl, sometimes incubates its eggs in warm volcanic ash!

It's the male's job to make sure the mound stays the right temperature. He keeps testing the temperature with his long tongue, and adding or removing material as needed. He keeps the temperature steady at just about 91° F (33° C). Even though a mallee fowl is only about as big as a rooster, one male can move about 150 tons of material to create a mound. It may be 5 feet (1.5 m) high and 10 feet (3 m) wide!

After 7 or 8 weeks, the newly hatched young mallee fowl scratch their way up to the surface. Unlike most birds, they can fend for themselves right from the start. In less than 24 hours, they head off on their own. The father's work is done—until next year.

The Emperor Penguin

The big emperor penguin of the Antarctic doesn't build any sort of nest at all. It would be hard to find good nest-making materials in the Antarctic's frozen landscape! Even without a nest, the emperor penguin manages to breed and lay its eggs in the middle of the brutal polar winter.

After two penguins mate, the female lays a single egg. The male balances the egg on his feet and drapes a fold of his belly over it. The female waddles off to the ocean to feed, leaving the male to warm the egg.

For more than 2 months the male stands warming the egg through ice storms and blizzards. Sometimes it gets so cold that several males huddle together for warmth. During this time, the male hardly moves and doesn't eat at all.

Finally the egg begins to hatch, and the mother returns—just in time. She recognizes her mate by his special nasal calls. She has spent these months feeding and getting fat, and now she vomits partially digested food stored in her **crop** for the hatchling to eat.

Finally, the scrawny male gets to waddle off to find some food. He stays in the ocean for a few weeks building himself up by eating fish and squid. Then he returns to help raise the chick.

An emperor penguin feeds its hungry chick.

No other bird lays its eggs in the dead of winter—especially an Antarctic winter. By laying their eggs so early in the year, emperor penguins give their young a head start. The young need all spring, summer, and fall to grow big and strong to survive the next winter.

Eggs in a Burrow

Many other species of penguins nest in burrows along the seashore. The Magellanic penguins of Argentina nest in huge colonies of up to 700,000 birds. Each pair makes a burrow, and the female lays two eggs in it. The first chick to hatch is bigger and gets more of the food its parents bring. The smaller chick often dies.

Penguins can't fly, and they look a bit comical waddling about on the ice. Sometimes, they lie down on their bellies and slide along the ice. In the ocean, however, they are strong and smooth, graceful swimmers, "flying" through the water with ease. They are protected from the icy waters by a thick layer of fat. In their hunt for **prey**, they can dive as deep as 870 feet (265 m).

A colony of oilbirds in their cave.

Chapter Four

What a Strange Way to Act!

Some birds just don't behave the way birds are "supposed" to. Not all birds perch prettily or soar gracefully. Imagine finding huge flocks of birds spending their days like bats in dark caves. Picture newly hatched chicks that jump out of trees and into the water when danger threatens. Can you imagine a bird that's such a clumsy flier that it may crash into trees when it tries to fly? Oilbirds, hoatzin, and tinamous are among the oddest birds in the world!

The Odd Oilbird

In the eighteenth century, an explorer named Alexander von Humboldt went into a dark cave in Venezuela. Suddenly, the air was filled with loud shrieks and screams. He felt hundreds of creatures swooping around his head. Were they some kind of strange bats? In the darkness, the noise was deafening and terrifying!

Later, von Humboldt learned from the local people that the creatures he had heard were actually oilbirds. These cave-dwelling birds feed on oily fruits of palm trees found near their caves.

Oilbirds spend the day in huge, noisy flocks in dark caves. The birds can't digest the seeds of the fruits they eat, so the cave floor is covered with piles of seeds that they have thrown up. To find their way around in the darkness, they make clicking noises that bounce off the walls. By listening to the time it takes their clicks to bounce back off of objects, the birds can tell when there's an object ahead. Oilbirds are the only birds

Light from a Bird?

Eating oily palm fruits makes the flesh of the oilbirds oily too. In fact, the people near the caves used to trap the oilbirds and boil them down for the oil, which they used for cooking and for filling their lamps. Imagine a bird-powered lamp!

that use **echolocation** the way that bats do. They are also the only nocturnal fruit-eating birds in the world. When they come out at night, they use their extremely keen vision to find their way through the trees.

Oilbirds are strange in other ways too. Most birds use nests only in breeding season to keep their eggs and young safe, but oilbirds come back to their nests every day to roost. These nests are made of mounds of **regurgitated** seeds piled on cave ledges. The nests grow bigger every year.

After the young hatch, the adults bring them the same oily fruits that they feed on themselves. These rich fruits make the young very fat. Seventy days after hatching, they are much bigger than the adults are! As their feathers grow in, though, they gradually lose weight, until they are the same size as the adults. Then they are ready to fly off in the darkness by themselves.

The Curious Hoatzin

Newly hatched birds are supposed to stay in their nests until they're ready to fly, aren't they? Not the hoatzin chicks! They are born with sparse down on their bodies and two claws on each leathery wing. While the chicks are waiting for the adults to bring home a beakful of leaves for them to eat, they clamber about in the branches, holding on with their claws.

Hoatzin build nests in bushes overhanging the water. When danger threatens, the young leap out of the bushes to land with a splash in the water below. They're not stuck down

Hoatzin are prehistoric-looking birds.

there forever though. As soon as the coast is clear, the young hoatzin climb back up into the bushes.

Hoatzin are the only tree-living birds that feed their young leaves rather than insects. The adults are strict vegetarians too. They have a huge **crop** that weighs one-third the weight of their whole body. They need this large crop to crush the leaves that they eat.

Although these South American birds have big wings, they aren't very good fliers. They spend most of their time on the ground or perched in bushes. When they do fly, they rarely travel more than 150 feet (45 m). The local people call hoatzin "stinking pheasants," because they look a bit like pheasants and they have a nasty smell. That bad smell is their only defense against **predators**, but it works.

The Solitary Tinamou

The tinamou of South America is related to the rhea, but it looks more like a chicken. Unlike the rhea, the tinamou has well-developed flight muscles, and it can fly—but not too well. A tinamou is so clumsy in the air that it often slams into trees or rocks. It may even kill itself in a crash!

The tinamou roosts in trees at night, but it has a hard time holding on. So, instead of perching, it squats lengthwise on a thick branch. Its legs are covered with rough scales that help the tinamou keep its grip on the branch.

Tinamous are better off staying on the ground—but they have trouble there too. Although they have well-developed

Claws on its Wings?

The young of some other bird species, including European coots, also have claws on their wings that help them climb.

Solitary tinamous are better off on the ground.

legs for running, they tire easily. If an enemy chases a tinamou for long, the bird soon becomes exhausted and begins stumbling awkwardly.

This bird's best defense is **camouflage**. It can sit still in the underbrush with its head stretched up and blend in perfectly with its surroundings. If an enemy comes too close, the

tinamou slips quietly away through the undergrowth or hides in a hole.

Like the rhea, the male tinamou may mate with many females. Each female lays her eggs in the male's nest. The male then guards the eggs and cares for the young alone. When he needs to go off to eat, he may cover the nest with leaves, but mostly he relies on his camouflage to protect the eggs. If you come upon a nesting tinamou, he will stay put on his nest. You might not even see him!

The meat of a tinamou is strange-looking. It's nearly transparent, but it's delicious. The local people who hunt tinamous for food have a hard time finding them, because they move so quietly and are so good at hiding. Tinamous may seem like clumsy birds, but they survive quite nicely!

A rhinoceros hornbill's bill looks way too big!

Chapter Five

Weird Beaks and Feathers

A bird flying through the air is much better off with a lightweight bill than with heavy jaws. A bird's bill is adapted for flying as well as for feeding. Yet some birds have very unusual bills, including really huge ones. You might wonder how these birds can manage to get off the ground!

Strong but lightweight feathers are another adaptation for flight. The various types of feathers on a bird's wings and body, including flight feathers and tail feathers, help to make some birds superb flying machines. Some birds have other feather adaptations that are just right for the life they lead. Ducks and geese, for instance, have oil on their feathers for waterproofing. That allows them to spend time in the water without getting their feathers too wet and heavy to fly. Keeping the water out with water-proofing also keeps the birds warm.

Other birds, though, have feathers that seem all wrong. Some male birds have strange, extra-long feathers that couldn't possibly help them fly. Some birds that spend most of their time in the water don't have waterproof feathers. There's a reason for these strange adaptations, though.

When it comes to beaks and feathers, some birds break all the rules.

The Nosy Toucan

The toco toucan of South America looks more like a bird body attached to a beak than the other way around. It looks as though the bird is *all* beak! How can the toucan fly carrying that huge thing around?

Actually, a toucan's beak isn't as heavy as it looks. Inside the thin, horny sheath, the bill is hollow except for crisscrossed

bony rods that help support and strengthen it. A toucan's beak is actually fairly fragile and can break easily.

Why does it need such a big beak? The toucan's beak helps it get the fruit it likes to eat. This heavy bird can sit safely on a big, strong branch and use its beak to reach far out for fruit

The toucan's colorful bill is just right for reaching far-off food.

41

growing on the ends of thinner branches. It plucks the fruit with the tip of its bill and tosses it back into its throat.

The oversized beak also has another use. Sometimes a toucan eats bird eggs or chicks. When a toucan suddenly appears at a nest with that huge, brightly colored beak, the adult birds are too terrified to fight back. The toucan grabs its prey and flies off, leaving the adults with one less mouth to feed.

These beautiful birds are often captured and sold in pet stores, and many die on the way. Sad to say, there are fewer toucans in the wild than there used to be.

The Skimmer's Scoop

A skimmer's bill looks very strange. The lower part is much longer than the top part! At first glance you might think a skimmer is deformed, but that unique beak is well suited to a skimmer's fishing method.

The lower part of the skimmer's bill is narrow and flattened like a knife's blade. A skimmer flies rapidly just above the surface of the water, with its lower beak plowing through the water. When it feels a small fish, the skimmer snaps it up in its

A black skimmer's bill is perfect for skim-fishing.

Plenty of Skimmers

Skimmers are very successful fishers. There are only three species of skimmers, but you can find them along oceans, lakes, and rivers from the eastern United States all the way to the tip of South America, in Africa, and in Asia.

scissor-like bill. Sometimes a skimmer mal over the same spot to snap up any fish that first time around.

A skimmer has other adaptations that sui bird feeds at dusk and all through the night. mer hunt, it has eyes like a cat. A skimmer is eyes like that. The vertical **pupils** help it : light. A skimmer also has very long wings— the length of its body—so it is a very good flier. Those long wings help the bird stay level as it flies low over the surface of the water.

Young skimmers start running around the beach only 2 days after they hatch, hunting for tasty tidbits. At first, both parts of their bills are the same size, but when they're old enough to skim the waters, they develop the same odd beaks as their parents.

The Swimming Cormorant

Cormorants swim along with their bodies underwater and only their heads showing. If you saw one, you might think it was a snake in the water. Why doesn't it swim on the top of the water like a duck?

44

Although they spend most of their time in the water, cormorants don't have waterproofing on their feathers, as ducks and swans do. Their feathers have spaces between them that let water in and air out. This arrangement helps these birds to sink and dive easily.

Cormorants dive as deep as 165 feet (50 m) chasing after fish. Everything about them is made for diving. Their legs are set way back on their bodies, so that they can propel themselves

Only its head shows when a double-crested cormorant goes swimming.

along with their webbed feet. When they press their wings to their sides they are perfectly streamlined. They have many blood vessels in their body that can hold a lot of oxygen, so that they can stay underwater for a long time without coming up for air.

Out of water, though, cormorants are clumsy. They waddle along on legs meant for swimming. You may see a cormorant roosting in a tree with its wings spread out. It's trying to dry its soaking-wet feathers!

There are about thirty species of cormorants living in many parts of the world, including the Americas, Europe, Asia, Africa, and even near Antartica.

The Lyrebird's Display

You may have seen birds with strange tails, but the male superb lyrebird of Australia seems to have gone completely overboard! He has a long, beautiful tail—longer than the rest of his body—made up of many different kinds of feathers. He holds it horizontally over his back, drooped over his head like a

A male superb lyrebird showing off his fancy tail.

big fan. The gracefully curved outer feathers of his tail look like the ancient Greek harp called a lyre.

The lyrebird's spectacular tail helps the male attract females. He sets up a big territory of 6 to 8 acres (2.5 to 3 hectares) and builds as many as 20 mounds of dirt. Then, standing on a mound or a stump, he does a fantastic dance. First, he circles slowly around, singing a loud song. A female can hear him from 2600 feet (800 m) away!

When a female comes close, the male holds his tail forward and quivers it rapidly, making a strange clicking call. At the height of his display, he glides back and forth around the female, then leaps back and forth over and over. In time with his leaping, he sings a rhythmic song that ends in two bell-like notes. If he's lucky, the female is completely won over by this amazing display!

A male mates with several females, and each female goes off to build a domed nest— a sort of earthen igloo. The female lyrebird takes care of the eggs alone. During the morning, she leaves the nest for 3 to 6 hours at a time, so that she can feed. The temperature of the eggs falls while she's away. That explains why the young take so long to hatch. The incubation period of lyrebird eggs may be as long as 6 weeks.

Lyrebirds spend most of their time on the ground scratching for insects. They are not very good fliers. To get up into a tree to roost, they jump from branch to branch. In the morning they glide gently down to the forest floor.

The Peacock's Tail

Like the male lyrebird, the peacock also uses his long feathers to attract females. His enormous tail fan is made of two hundred dazzling feathers.

Lyrebirds hide in dense undergrowth, so they are hard to spot—but you can't miss their loud songs. The males can mimic the songs of other birds perfectly. A single male lyrebird can copy the songs of as many as sixteen other birds. He can also mimic the barking of dogs, train whistles, and even the beep of a car horn!

The world of birds can be full of surprises!

Chapter Six

Fine Feathered Finale

The world of birds is full of oddities! So many birds break the "rules" that you may start wondering what the rules really are. It's true that all birds have feathers, but several couldn't fly if their lives depended on it. Many other birds just don't look—or behave—the way you might expect.

Now that you know about some of these very unusual birds, you may have a different idea about what a bird is. The next time someone asks you, "What is a bird?" you could confidently say that "All birds are warm-blooded vertebrates with feathers." Then the definitions get harder. You might say, "*Most* birds are adapted for flying," and "*Most* birds have lightweight beaks." You might add that "*Most* birds have a poor sense of smell," and "*Most* birds care for their eggs and young in a nest."

Then, you might want to go on to describe the appearance and behavior of some of the unusual birds that break all the rules. The world of birds is full of surprises!

Bizarre Birds Around the World

Common name	Scientific name	Where found
Bee hummingbird	*Mellisuga helenae*	Cuba
Ostrich	*Struthio camelus*	Sahara, Somalia, Ethiopia, and parts of East Africa and Zambesi
Kiwi	family Apterygidae, (three species)	New Zealand and nearby small islands
Greater rhea	*Rhea americana*	South America
Jacanas	*Jacanidae* spp. (eight species)	Africa, India, Southeast Asia, New Guinea, Australia, the Americas, and West Indies
Shaft-tailed whydah	*Tetraenura regia*	Africa
Mallee fowl	*Leipoa ocellata*	Australia
Emu	*Dromaius novaehollandiae*	Australia
Emperor penguin	*Aptenodytes forsteri*	Antarctica
Magellanic penguin	*Spheniscus magellanicus*	Argentina
Oilbird	*Steatornis caripensis*	Venezuela, other parts of South America, Trinidad
Hoatzin	*Opisthocomus hoatzin*	Jungles of Amazon River valley
Toco toucan	*Ramphastos toco*	Eastern South America
Rhinoceros hornbill	*Buceros rhinoceros*	Malay Peninsula and several East Indies islands
Skimmer	*Rynchops* spp. (three species)	All around the world—in the Americas, Africa, and Asia

continued next page

Bizarre Birds Around the World _continued_

Common name	Scientific name	Where found
Cormorant	_Phalacrocorax_ spp.	Americas, Europe, Asia, Africa, and even near Antarctica
Anhinga	_Anhinga_ spp.	Mainly southeastern USA
Superb lyrebird	_Menura novaehollandiae_	Australia
Common peafowl (male:peacock. female:peahen)	_Pavo cristatus_	India, Sri Lanka, Burma, Java. Ceylon, Malaya
Congo peafowl	_Afropavo congensis_	Democratic Republic of Congo in Africa

Glossary

casque—a helmet-like structure on top of some birds' heads

camouflage—blending into the surroundings to hide. Some animals have developed special coloring or body shapes to help camouflage themselves.

class—a group of animals that share certain characteristics. Birds are in the class *aves*.

clutch—several eggs laid at the same time in a nest

crop—a pouch in a bird's throat where it stores and grinds its food

echolocation—a way certain animals find their way about by bouncing sounds off of objects

endangered—when there is a risk of a species becoming extinct

extinction—when there are no living members of a species

embryo—an unborn animal in an early stage of development inside its mother or its egg

evolved—changed slowly over time

incubation period—the time it takes a newly laid egg to hatch

keel—a raised bony structure on a bird's breastbone that its flight muscles are attached to

pupils—the black part of the eye that lets light through

predator—an animal that hunts another animal

prey—an animal hunted by another animal for food

regurgitate—to throw up food; to vomit

vertebrae—the bones that make up the backbone

vertebrates—animals with a backbone

warm-blooded—an animal that can regulate its own internal body temperature

yolk sac—a sac of nutrients that birds feed on as embryos and sometimes also after they hatch

To Find Out More

Books

Baskin-Salzberg, Anita and Allen Salzberg. *Flightless Birds*. Danbury, CT: Franklin Watts, 1993.

Lovett, Sarah. *Extremely Weird Birds*. Santa Fe: NM: John Muir Publications, 1996.

Ollason, Robert J. *Penguin Parade*. Minneapolis, MN: Lerner Publications, 1995.

Schlein, Miriam. *What's a Penguin Doing in a Place Like This?* Brookfield, CT: Millbrook Press.

Stevens, Ann Shepard. *Strange Nests*. Brookfield, CT: Millbrook Press, 1998.

Stotsky, Sandra. *Birds, Birds, Birds*. Broomall, PA: Chelsea House, 1998.

Taylor, Barbara. *Bird Atlas*. New York: Knopf, 1993.

Wallace, Ian. *Mysteries and Marvels of Bird Life*. Tulsa, OK: EDC Publications, 1986.

Wechsler, Doug. *Bizarre Birds*. Honesdale, PA: Boyds Mills Press, 1999.

Organizations and Online Sites

The Animal Diversity Web
http://www.oit.itd.umich.edu/bio/
This site contains information about individual species in several different classes of animals.

Animals–Australia
http://www.ozramp.net.au/~senani/animaust.htm
This is a site devoted to Australian animals, including kiwis.

The Audubon Society
http://www.audubon.org
This organization is an amazing source of information for people interested in birds and birdwatching.

GeoZoo: Earth Safari

http://www.geobop.com/geozoo/

This site offers GeoReports, GeoCharts, and quick facts about a wide variety of animals.

Penguins Aplenty!

http://www.milner.coos-bay.k12.or.us/home/penguins.htm

This site provides links to other sites for people interested in learning about penguins.

U.S. Fish and Wildlife Service

http://www.fws.gov

This United States government agency has information on endangered species, habitat conservation, and more.

A Note on Sources

The first thing I did when I began work on this book was to dig into my memory. Over the years, I have taken numerous courses in natural history and visited dozens of zoos and nature preserves around the world. Thinking about those experiences gave me more ideas for strange birds to include.

My next step was to browse through my personal nature library for ideas and facts. I started with Garth Harrison's *Birds of the World*, a handbook with pictures and information on many birds. Christopher Perrin's *The Encyclopedia of Birds* and Joseph Forshaw's *Encyclopedia of Birds* both proved to be excellent resource books.

Finally, once I knew which species I wanted to include, I went to the Internet. Two especially helpful sites are *The Animal Diversity Web* and *GeoZoo: Earth Safari*.

The help of expert consultant Kathy Carlstead, Ph.D., of the Honolulu Zoo in Honolulu, Hawaii, was invaluable in creating this book. —*Sara Swan Miller*

Index

Numbers in *italics* indicate illustrations.

Africa, birds in, 19, 23, 44, 46, 53–54

Americas (North and South), birds in, 23, 44, 46, 53–54

Anhinga, 46, 54

Antarctic, birds in, 27, 46, 53–54

Asia, birds in, 23, 44, 46, 53–54

Australia, birds in, 14, 23, 46, 53–54

Bald eagle, *20*

Bats, 33

Beak, 13, 39, 40–44
  hornbill, 42
  kiwi, 13–14
  skimmer, 42–44
  toucan, 40–42

Bee hummingbird, 9, 53

Camouflage of tinamou, 36–37

Cave-dwelling birds, 32

Claws on wings, 33, 35

Common peafowl, 54

Congo peafowl, 54

Cormorant, 44–45, *45*, 46, 54

Cuckoo, 25

Diet of birds
  hoatzin, 35
  kiwi, 12
  lyrebird, 48
  oilbirds, 32
  ostrich, 19
  skimmer, 42–44
  toucan, 41–42

Ducks, 40

Echolocation, 33

Eggs. *See* Nesting habits

Elephant bird, 19
Emperor penguin, 27–28, *28*, 29, 53
Emu, 14, *14*, 53
Europe, birds in, 35, 46, 53–54
European coots, 35
Eyesight of birds, 9, 44
Extinction, birds facing, 16, 17, 19

Feathers, unusual
  cormorant, 45
  lyrebird, 46–49
  peacock, 49
  shaft-tailed whydah, 24–25
  types of, 39–40
Flightless birds, 11–19, 29
  advantages and disadvantages, 17
  cormorant, 44–46
  kiwi, 12
  ostrich, 17–19
  penguin, 29
  rhea, 14–17
Flying birds, 8–9, 10, 35, 42

Geese, 40
Greater rhea. *See* Rhea

Hoatzin, 31–32, 33, *34*, 35, 53
Hornbill, 38, *38*, 42, 53

India, birds in, 23, 53–54

Jacana, 22, *22*, 23, 53

Keel, 9, 12
Kiwi, 12–13, *13*, 14, 17, 53

"Lily trotters." *See* Pheasant-tailed jacana
Locations, 53–54
Lyrebird, 46, *47*, 48–49, 54

Magellanic penguins, 29, *29*, 53
Mallee fowl, 25–26, *26*, 27, 53
Mating habits
  jacana, 23
  lyrebird, 48
  rhea, 16
  tinamou, 37

Names (common and scientific), 53–54
Nesting habits
  common scrub fowl, 26

cuckoo, 25
hoatzin, 33
jacana, 22
kiwi, 14
lyrebird, 48
mallee fowl, 25–27
oilbird, 32–33
ostrich, 19
penguins, 27–28, 29
shaft-tailed whydah, 23
tinamou, 37
New Guinea, birds in, 23,
    53–54
New Zealand, birds in, 12, 53
Nocturnal birds, 12, 33, 44

Oilbird, *30*, 31–33, 53
Ostrich, *8*, 11, 17–18, *18*, 19,
    53

Peacock, 49, 54
Penguin, 27–29, 53
Pheasant-tailed jacana, 22,
    22, 23

Rhea, 14, 15, *15*, 16, *16*, 17,
    35, 37, 53
Rhinoceros hornbill, 38, *38*,
    42, 53
Robin, *6*, 11

Scientific names, 53–54
Scrub fowl, 26
Shaft-tailed whydah, 23–24,
    24, 25, 53
Skimmer, 42, *43*, 44, 53
Solitary tinamou, 35–37
Sounds, unusual
    lyrebird, 49
    oilbird, 32
South America, birds in, 14,
    35, 40, 53–54
Southeast Asian birds, 23, 53
"Stinking pheasants." *See*
    Hoatzin

Tinamou, 32, 35–36, *36*, 37
Toco toucan, 40–41, *41*, 42,
    53

Venezuela, birds in, 32,
    53–54
Violet-eared waxbills, 23
von Humboldt, Alexander,
    32

Wings, unusual
    European coot, 35
    hoatzin, 33
    skimmer, 44
Woodpecker, *10*

About the Author

Sara Swan Miller has enjoyed working with children all her life, first as a Montessori nursery-school teacher and later as an outdoor environmental educator at the Mohonk Preserve in New Paltz, New York. As director of the school program, she has taught hundreds of children the importance of appreciating and respecting the natural world.

She has written more than 30 books, including *Three Stories You Can Read to Your Dog; Three Stories You Can Read to Your Cat; Three More Stories You Can Read to Your Dog;* and *What's in the Woods? An Outdoor Activity Book;* as well as four other books on strange animals for the Watts Library. She has also written several True Books on farm animals for Children's Press, and more than a dozen books for Franklin Watts' *Animals in Order* series.